The <u>most</u> <u>excellent</u> book of
fancy dress

Moe Casey

Aladdin / Watts

LONDON • SYDNEY

© Aladdin Books Ltd 1997

Designed and produced by
Aladdin Books Ltd
28 Percy Street
London
WIP 0LD

ISBN 0 7496 2705 0

*First published in
Great Britain in 1997 by*
**Aladdin Books/
Watts Books**
96 Leonard Street
London
EC2A 4RH

Editor
Sarah Levete

Design

David West
CHILDREN'S BOOK DESIGN
Designer
Robert Perry
Illustrator
Rob Shone

Picture Research
Brooks Krikler Research

646.4706

049-627-050 4528

CONTENTS

INTRODUCTION

Throughout history, people across the world have dressed in costumes for different purposes. Nations and races can be identified by their dress. Disguises allow people to act out different characters – for instance, court jesters were allowed to say things to kings that other people would have been punished for. Dressing up is fashionable at masked balls *(above right)*, carnivals *(above left)*, festivals *(below right)* and parties. This book gives you the chance to make imaginative costumes using easily available materials. Try out different characters and think of some designs of your own.

As you read the book, look for these symbols:
★ *tells you what specific materials and equipment you will need for the costume;*
✔ *gives you tips on how to perfect your costume and how to act out a character to suit your fancy dress.*

Different MATERIALS

Start collecting different and unusual materials.

★ Collect old *wrapping paper; food packaging; bottle tops; straws; bubble wrap; coloured plastic tops; cardboard boxes; plastic bottles; rubber gloves; old clothes or pieces of material such as net, fake fur and felt; scarves; and baseball caps. You may need to buy: cotton balls; coloured cellophane, tissue and crepe paper; stick-on velcro; and wadding or foam (from a needlecraft or department store). Don't worry if you don't have a particular item – most of the materials can be replaced – just think of an alternative.*

Examples of the types of materials which you can collect and use.

Safety first

• Use non-toxic pva glue and non-toxic acryllic paint • be careful when you use scissors – if you have difficulty, ask an adult to help • avoid putting glitter near your eyes • when you staple things, put some tape behind the sharp edges of the staple • make sure your face is never covered completely by plastic or foam • if you are uncomfortable in a costume, take it off and make some alterations •

★ *For each costume, have the following to hand: scissors; stapler and staples; pva glue; Sellotape; parcel tape or masking tape; ruler; needle and thread; and a paintbrush.*

The long edges of a cardboard box are called the front and back; the short edges are called the sides. If you need to cut out the base of a box and your box has open flaps, just cut off the flaps.

Cleaning up

Cover your work area with newspaper and clean up when you have finished.

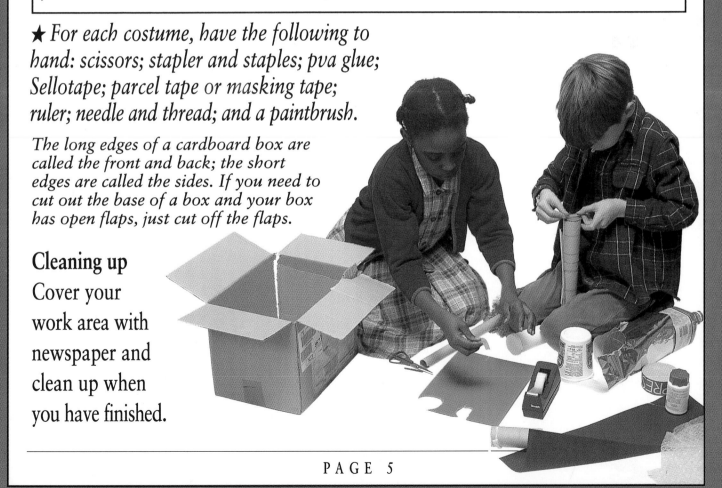

Putting things TOGETHER

Simple techniques to help you make some of the costumes

Pattern-making grid

To make a pattern from a grid, cover paper or card with 2 cm squared boxes *(left)*, or buy paper printed with 2 cm squares. Copy the pattern on the grid shown in the drawing for the costume, by matching the pattern on the squares with your squared paper *(below)*. This will enlarge it. Cut out the pattern.

Template

Use tracing paper to copy your grid pattern onto card. Trace the outline in pencil; turn the tracing paper over (pencil side face down on the grid); and trace through the original line. Lift the tracing paper off; draw over the faint outline, and cut out. Use this template to draw around to make other copies.

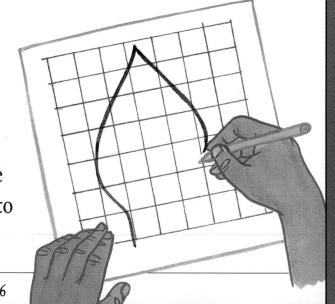

Scoring

This is when you drag the point of the scissors along a straight line next to a ruler (*right*). Scoring cuts card just on the surface, making it easier to bend. This is used on the "colourful sweet" (*see pages 10-11*).

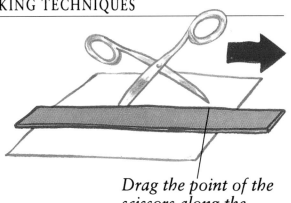

Drag the point of the scissors along the edge of the ruler

Oversewing

Right side

This is sewing over two edges. Place two pieces of fabric with their right sides together. The needle is then put through both pieces and the thread pulled tight and then repeated (*left*). This is used on the "furry alien" (*see pages 22-23*).

Wrong side

Gathering stitch

This is a large flat stitch which is pulled in to form gathers (*right*). This is used for the "superhero" cape (*see pages 18-19*).

Gathers form as the stitch is pulled in

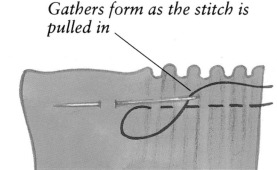

✔ *If you find a technique difficult, ask an adult for help. Read through the instructions carefully before you begin making your costume.*

Beautiful BUTTERFLY

Flap your wings gracefully like a butterfly!

★ *Large cardboard box;
2 lengths of 1 cm wide
elastic; glitter;
newspaper; coloured
tissue paper; and paint.*

1 Cut the front and back out of
the cardboard box.

2 Draw a half butterfly wing shape
(*right*) onto newspaper; make sure it
will cover the top half of your body.
Cut this out and trace around it on the two pieces of
cardboard. Cut out a pair of wings.

3 Lay the wings next to each other. Add a little
water to some glue. Brush this onto the
front of the wings. Cover each
wing with tissue paper. Glue on crushed
tissue paper.

4 Cut a strip
of card to cover
the inner
wing
edges.

5

*Cotton ball
dipped in
glitter*

*Elastic strips
for your arms*

✔ *Why not make a caterpillar costume to wear before you are transformed into a butterfly? Have a look at some pictures or photos of caterpillars to give you some ideas.*

5 Score and fold and down the centre of this strip. Glue and tape it to the back of the wings.

6 Paint the back of the wings. Staple the elastic strips onto the front of the wings. Your arms fit through here.

7 Place the wings on the newspaper and paint glue onto the edge of the wings. Sprinkle a little glitter around, shaking off the excess. Repeat this a few times.

Headband and springs

8 Ask an adult to help you put your wings on. Wear coloured leggings and a leotard or sweater.

★ *For the antennae, attach two painted pipe cleaners, straws or springs to an old hairband. Stick a cotton ball on top of each. Paint them with pva glue and dip them into a bag of glitter. Shake off the excess onto some newspaper. Do this several times to cover the balls in glitter.*

EXCELLENT SWEET COSTUME

Colourful SWEET

Smile sweetly...

1 Cut a hole large enough for your head in the top of the small box. Cut out the base or its flaps. In the sides of the box, cut two shoulder grooves.

★ *A roll of coloured cellophane; coloured wrapping paper; small cardboard box; large cardboard box; coloured paint; and stiff paper.*

2 Cut two oval shapes from the front and back of the large box. Cover them in wrapping paper. Tape them to the front and back of the small box.

3 From one side of the large box, cut a length 5 cm deep and 74 cm long. Draw a line 1.5 cm from its edge; score and fold along the line. Cut up to the fold at 1 cm intervals.

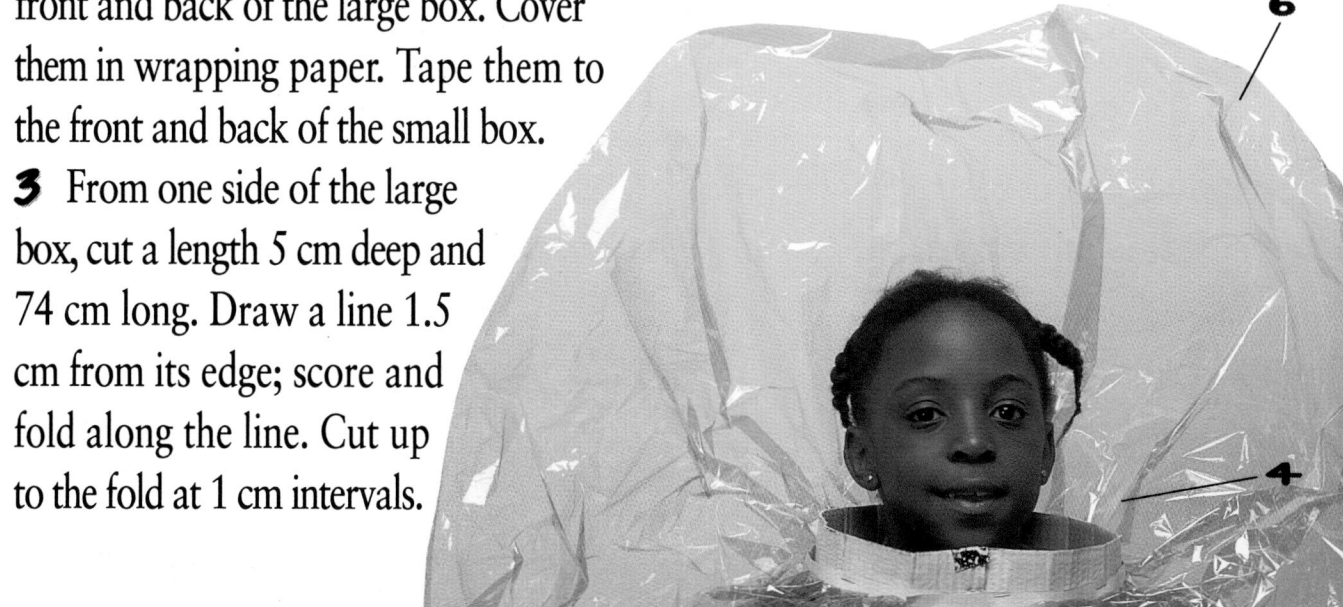

4 Paint this length the same colour as the cellophane paper. Staple it together to form a circle. Glue and tape this around the hole in the top of the small box.

5 Cut a length of card 5 cm deep and 91 cm long, to form a circle. Tape it around the bottom of both oval shapes.

6 Cut a length of paper 74 cm long and 2.5 cm deep. Make pleats in the cellophane (1 cm deep and 1 cm apart). Staple and tape the pleats along the edge of the paper. This is fiddly so you may need to ask an adult to help you. Staple this around the cardboard circle (**4**). Leave a space in the front of the cellophane for your face. Repeat for the bottom of the sweet, stapling the paper to the circle shape (**5**). Here, tape the cellophane together. Ask an adult to help you put it on.

✔ *Make sure your friends aren't tempted to unwrap you!*

NEVER cover your face with the cellophane; leave a large gap.

Vampire BAT

Bat around, and terrify your friends as you go!

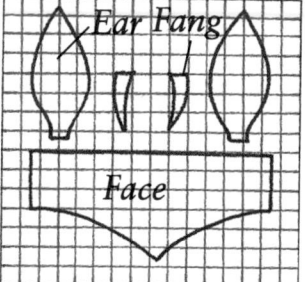

Ear Fang

Face

★ *Black baseball cap; black felt; black ribbon; black tracksuit or black top and trousers; black shoes; a large black bin bag; needle and strong thread; red paint; grid paper; and a small, thin piece of foam.*

1 Copy the ear and face patterns from the grid. Fold the felt in half and cut out two ear shapes. Sew the matching ear shapes together to make them double thickness. Cut out one face shape in black felt. Cut out foam fangs.

2 Cut 2 slits, 4 cm from the top of the baseball cap. Pleat the base of the ears; place one through each slit. Turn the cap inside out; sew ear in place.

3 Glue or stitch the felt face onto the back of the baseball cap. This is now the front. If glued, allow to dry.

Wrist and elbow ties

Ear

Front of baseball cap

Front of vampire face

Slit for ear

Fangs

Cut out eye shapes

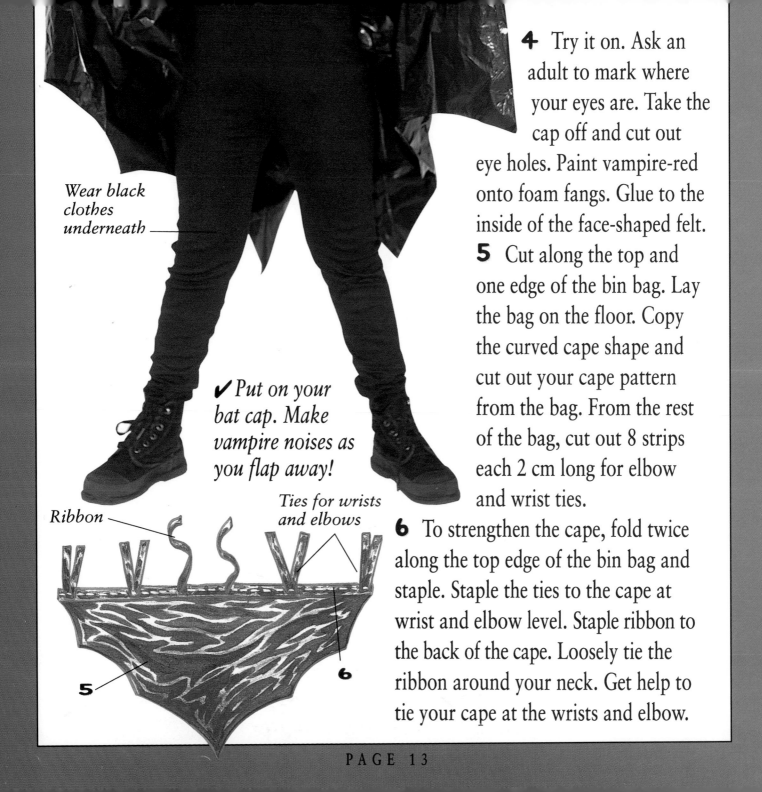

Wear black clothes underneath

✔ Put on your bat cap. Make vampire noises as you flap away!

Ribbon

Ties for wrists and elbows

4 Try it on. Ask an adult to mark where your eyes are. Take the cap off and cut out eye holes. Paint vampire-red onto foam fangs. Glue to the inside of the face-shaped felt.

5 Cut along the top and one edge of the bin bag. Lay the bag on the floor. Copy the curved cape shape and cut out your cape pattern from the bag. From the rest of the bag, cut out 8 strips each 2 cm long for elbow and wrist ties.

6 To strengthen the cape, fold twice along the top edge of the bin bag and staple. Staple the ties to the cape at wrist and elbow level. Staple ribbon to the back of the cape. Loosely tie the ribbon around your neck. Get help to tie your cape at the wrists and elbow.

EXCELLENT AMERICAN DINER COSTUME

American DINER

Wear your best smile. Have a nice day now!

★ *Grid sheet; 1 m of checked cloth or an old sheet painted with fabric paint; a large box; a paper plate; a baseball cap; an old bath sponge or foam; a piece of elastic for bow tie; and stick-on velcro.*

1 Cut out the base of the box and a semi-circle from the top. From the base cut a length for your waistband, 80 cm long and 8 cm wide.

2 Score a line 6 cm from the longer, top edge. Along the middle, cut up to the scored edge at 2 cm intervals. Bend the scored edges upwards. These edges fit under the semi-circle (stage **1**). Tape in place.

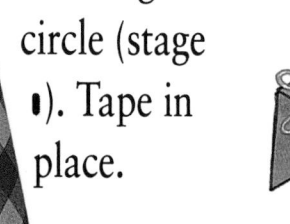

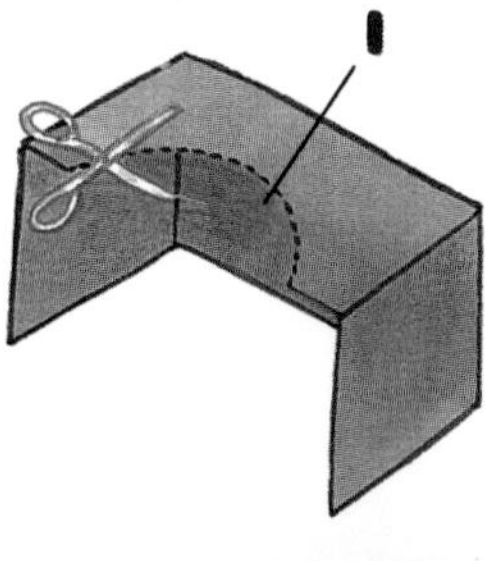

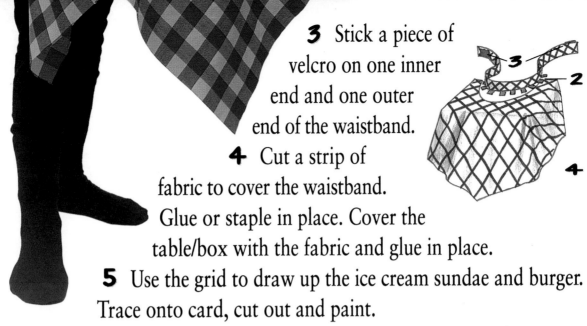

3 Stick a piece of velcro on one inner end and one outer end of the waistband.

4 Cut a strip of fabric to cover the waistband. Glue or staple in place. Cover the table/box with the fabric and glue in place.

5 Use the grid to draw up the ice cream sundae and burger. Trace onto card, cut out and paint.

6 Cut two slits in the top of the box and material. Push the ice cream base in one. Make a slit in the paper plate and push the burger through. Push this into the other table slit. Cut up an old bath sponge into chip shapes.

7 Cover the front of the baseball cap with some left-over material. Glue or sew in place. Make a bow tie by folding over a piece of the material into a rectangular shape. Pleat it in the centre and wrap a narrow piece of material around it. Thread some elastic behind the narrow piece. Ask an adult to tie it loosely around your neck and to attach the table at the back. Hold the table from underneath.

✔ *Have you got an order book and pen?*

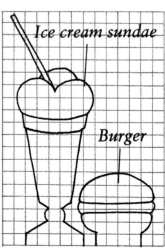

Ice cream sundae

Burger

Scary SKELETON

What a lot of bones!

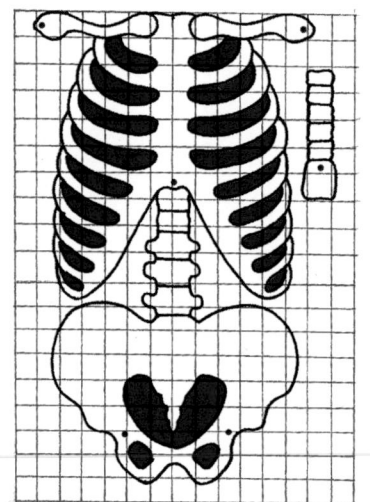

3

Rib cage and pelvis

★ *A large sheet of card (not too thick); a large grid sheet; paper fasteners; black paint and black felt-tips; white and black face paints; black elastic; ribbon or tape; black roll neck and leggings; and black gloves.*

1 Use the grid reference to make an enlarged skeleton pattern. You may need an adult to help you.

2 The bones are cut out using a template (*see page 6*). Draw around the template of the bone to make the other bones – you will need two of each of the bones to make two arms and two legs.

3 For the ribs and pelvis, cut the outer shape but mark out the gaps in between the bones with black felt-tip or paint.

4 Use the point of the scissors to make a hole, where the dots are marked.

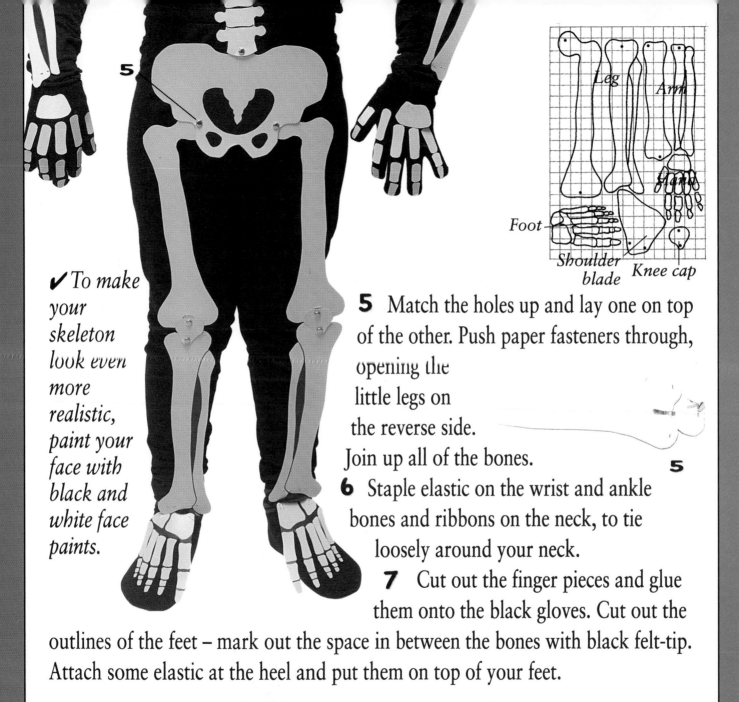

✔ *To make your skeleton look even more realistic, paint your face with black and white face paints.*

5 Match the holes up and lay one on top of the other. Push paper fasteners through, opening the little legs on the reverse side. Join up all of the bones.

6 Staple elastic on the wrist and ankle bones and ribbons on the neck, to tie loosely around your neck.

7 Cut out the finger pieces and glue them onto the black gloves. Cut out the outlines of the feet – mark out the space in between the bones with black felt-tip. Attach some elastic at the heel and put them on top of your feet.

✔ *Scrape your hair back with gel or wear a white headband.*

*Super*HERO

What superheroic deeds can you perform?

★ *Purple satin (140 cm wide, 1 m long); 2 fruit trays, from a greengrocer; a wide belt; cotton tape, 4 cm wide and long enough to go round your neck; baseball cap; red acryllic paint; newspaper; stick-on velcro; black elastic; and Wellington boots.*

1 Cut out one tray (as shown) for the front piece of your costume. For the headdress and boots, cut two corners off both trays.

Shape for front of costume

1

Cut 2 corners from each tray

2 From the other tray, cut two diagonal pieces for your wrist bands.

3 Put the pieces on some newspaper and paint them red on one side. Allow to dry and paint the other side.

4 Staple elastic to the wrist bands and boot pieces (two corners from stage **1**).

5 Staple the bottom of the front piece (**1**) to your belt.

Wrist band

Front piece

Belt

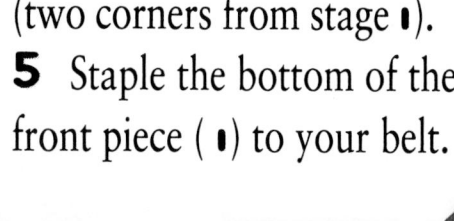

6 Stick two velcro pieces along the top edge of the front piece.

7 Cut the satin (for the cape) 70 cm long, using the whole width of fabric. Sew a gathering stitch across the top; pull it in to 50 cm; stitch this to some cotton tape. Stick a piece of velcro to each end of the cotton tape (this will attach to the velcro on your front piece). To stiffen the cape, lightly paint some pva glue along its bottom edge

8 Staple some material onto the baseball cap, the back of which will be the front.

Staple a headdress piece onto either side and staple a centre piece in the middle. With the elastic, attach the boot pieces to your Wellington boots.

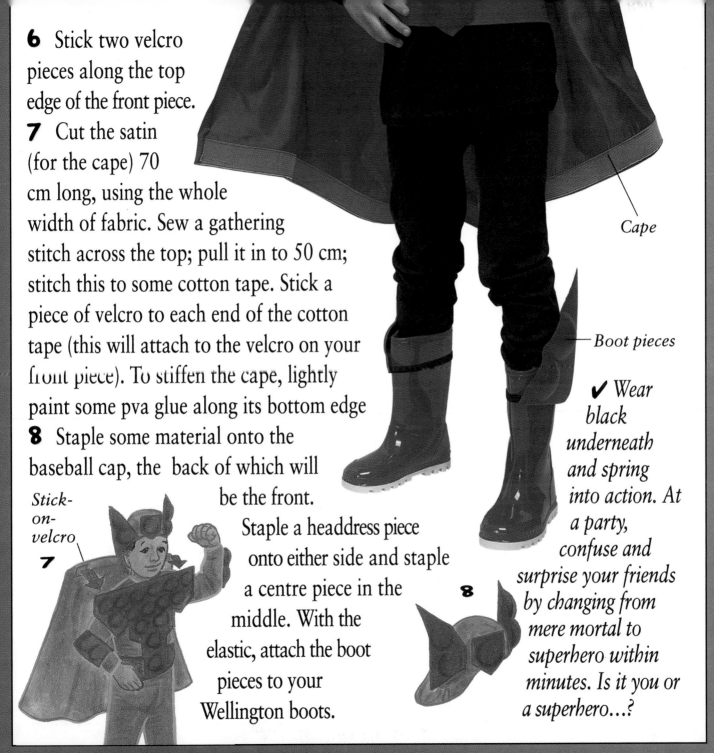

Cape

Boot pieces

Stick-on-velcro
7

8

✔ Wear black underneath and spring into action. At a party, confuse and surprise your friends by changing from mere mortal to superhero within minutes. Is it you or a superhero...?

Stinging JELLYFISH

Float around the party, stinging as you go.

★ A colander; plastic tubing cut into 2 lengths of 1 m and 1 length of 2 m (from an electrical shop); sheet or strips of bubble wrap; 1.5 m x 1.5 m of wadding or foam, 1 cm thick; old wool, thread, string or party throws; needle and thread; and blue and green paints.

1 Tape the 1 m tube lengths into a cross-shape.

2 Put the colander upside down on a stool. Tape the top of the cross onto the colander. Ask an adult to help you tape the 2 m length of tubing around the bottom of the cross.

Tube taped around 4 points of cross.

Colander

3 Place the wadding over the frame. Attach it by sewing the wadding to one of the cross shape pieces of tubing. Use big stitches.

Make sure you have cut a hole for your face.

4 Ask an adult to help you try it on and mark out a face shape. Take it off.

5 If the colander is too big, tape in extra wadding. Cut out the face shape.

6 Trim the wadding 3 cm below the tubing. From this, cut out strips for tentacles. Staple these to the bottom of the jellyfish.

7 Staple a sheet or strips of bubble wrap over the wadding. You could use cut-up plastic bags instead. Paint the bubble wrap or plastic bags in jellyfish colours. Staple on pieces of string, wool, thread or party throws.

8 Get someone to help you put it on.

Wear leggings or tracksuit and sweatshirt.

✔ *Practise floating or bobbing like a jelly-fish. Go to a party with the frog person (see page 29) but be careful with your sting!*

Hold the frame

EXCELLENT ALIEN COSTUME

Furry ALIEN

Alienate your friends!

Mask

1 Use the grid for the mask shape. Cut it out from the paper. Cut out eye holes. Staple some bubble wrap behind these holes.

2 Paint the mask and outline the eyes and edge. Paint dots on the bubble wrap. Staple thin fabric strips onto the lower edge of the mask. Sellotape the mask onto the bowl.

★ *Grid paper; piece of paper; a plastic bowl; 1 m of fur fabric or an old bed spread; 0.5 m of thin fabric cut into strips; 2 strips of wiro binding from old files, or pipe cleaners; old skirt or piece of material; 2 pairs of rubber gloves; green and black paint.*

Ask an adult to help you put the mask and collar on.

3 Place 2 strips of fur fabric (10 cm wide) across the top of the mask on the bowl. Into these, insert and staple wiro binding (antennae) to the fabric. Tie on material scraps.

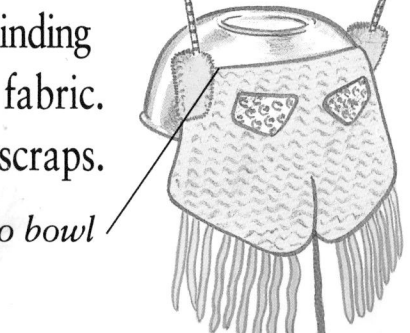

Sellotape mask to bowl

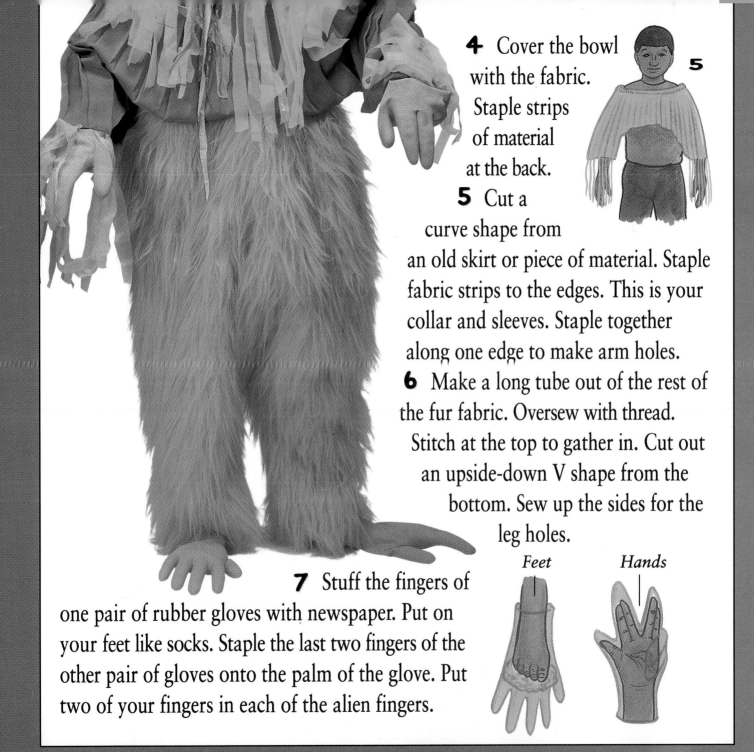

4 Cover the bowl with the fabric. Staple strips of material at the back.

5 Cut a curve shape from an old skirt or piece of material. Staple fabric strips to the edges. This is your collar and sleeves. Staple together along one edge to make arm holes.

6 Make a long tube out of the rest of the fur fabric. Oversew with thread. Stitch at the top to gather in. Cut out an upside-down V shape from the bottom. Sew up the sides for the leg holes.

Feet   *Hands*

7 Stuff the fingers of one pair of rubber gloves with newspaper. Put on your feet like socks. Staple the last two fingers of the other pair of gloves onto the palm of the glove. Put two of your fingers in each of the alien fingers.

EXCELLENT EGYPTIAN COSTUME

Elegant EGYPTIAN

Go back in time with this historical costume.

Sew wool across the tape

2

Put velcro along one inner and one outer edge of the collar's back opening. When you put it on, bend it slightly flat, so it does not stick out.

Snake shape

Collar

I Put the tights over your head (not your face). Tie the legs into a double knot. This is the wig base. Take it off; cut the tights off 6 cm away from the knot. Cut the cotton tape 4 cm longer than your head measurement from front to back.

2 Place the wool lengths on the cotton tape; sew the middle of the wool along the centre of the tape. Stitch and glue this to the wig base.

3 Paint a gold line on the bottom edge of the crepe paper. When dry, ask an adult to wrap it around your waist, pleating it at the front, and to staple it together.

4 Cut and paint 2 bracelets from gold card, 8 cm deep and 14 cm long.

Attach with stick-on velcro

6

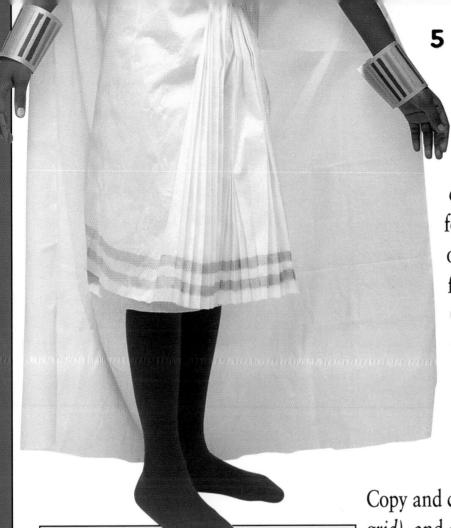

5 Copy and cut out the collar *(see grid)* onto plain card. Trace this 4 times (to make a circle) onto gold card. **4** Cut out; cut 1 side for the back opening; cut a circular hole for your neck. Paint the collar.

Stick-on velcro

6 Ask an adult to measure your head with the wig on. Cut a headband from the gold card, 4 cm wide and 3 cm longer than the measurement. Decorate it. Copy and cut out the snake shape *(see grid)*, and decorate. Staple this to the front of the headband.

7 Loosely tie white muslin at the neck, under your collar.

5

★ *100g ball thick black wool cut into lengths of 80 cm; old pair of black tights; 4 cm wide black cotton tape; needle and thread; white muslin (1.2 m); grid sheet; white crepe paper; large sheet of gold card; coloured paints; and stick-on velcro.*

EXCELLENT ROBOT COSTUME

Programmed ROBOT

What have you been programmed to do?

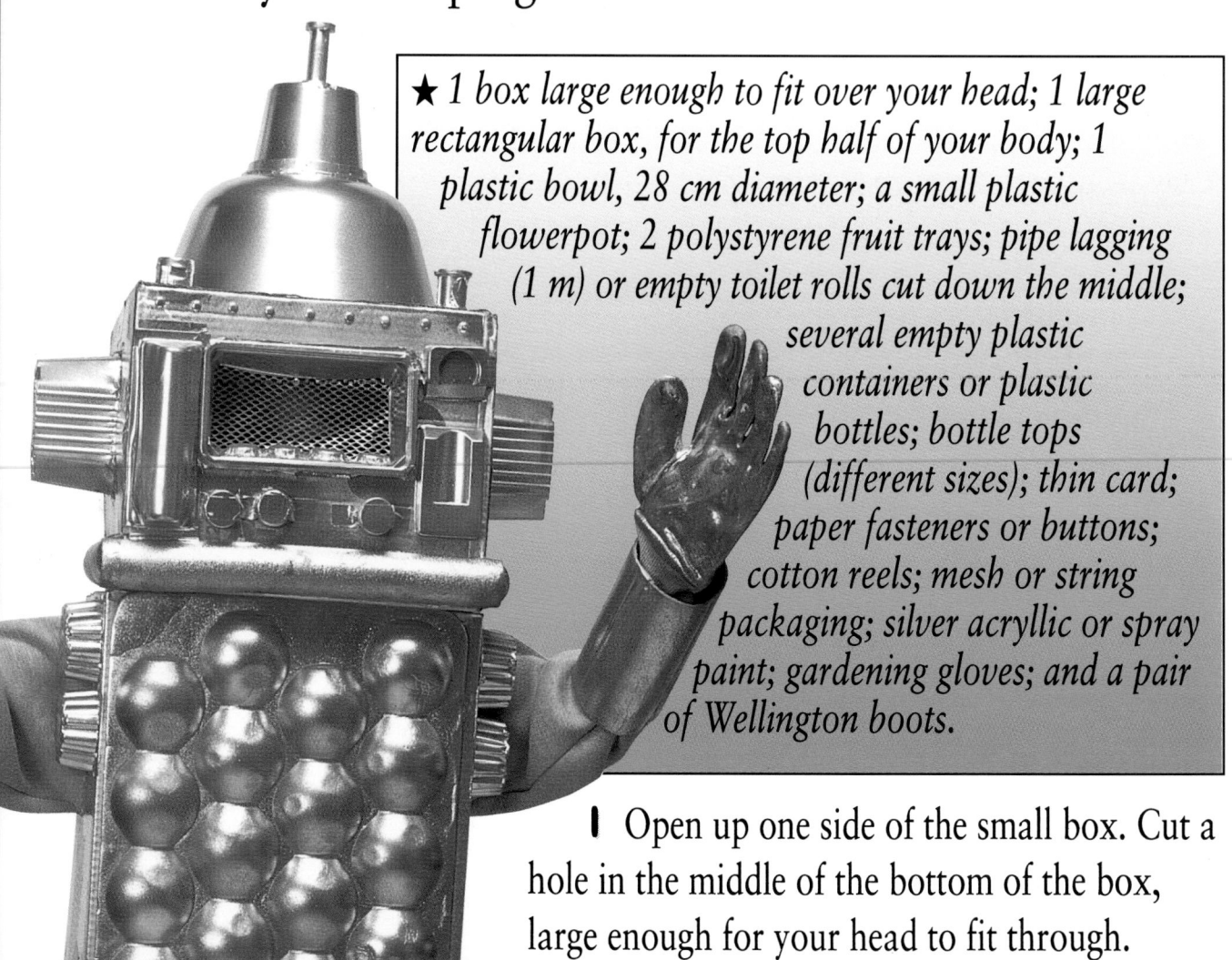

★ *1 box large enough to fit over your head; 1 large rectangular box, for the top half of your body; 1 plastic bowl, 28 cm diameter; a small plastic flowerpot; 2 polystyrene fruit trays; pipe lagging (1 m) or empty toilet rolls cut down the middle; several empty plastic containers or plastic bottles; bottle tops (different sizes); thin card; paper fasteners or buttons; cotton reels; mesh or string packaging; silver acryllic or spray paint; gardening gloves; and a pair of Wellington boots.*

I Open up one side of the small box. Cut a hole in the middle of the bottom of the box, large enough for your head to fit through.

2 In the front of the box, trace around a rectangular plastic container. Cut out the shape.

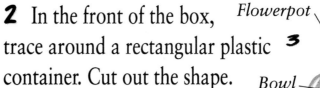

Flowerpot

Cotton reel

Bowl

Cartons

3 Trace around the plastic bowl on the top of the box and cut out the shape. Tape the flowerpot onto the top of the plastic bowl and tape a cotton reel on top of that.

4 Insert this through the inside of the box, pushing through the hole in the top. Tape firmly in place.

5 Tape and glue bottle tops and cotton reels either side of the bowl.

6 Cut the base off the rectangular plastic container. Tape some mesh or string packaging over the hole. Tape some bottle tops along the edge of the container. Paint it silver. This is now your eye hole. Decorate the top edge of the front of the box by inserting paper fasteners and sticking on buttons and bottle tops.

7 Insert your eye hole into the cut out rectangular shape (**2**) and tape it into place.

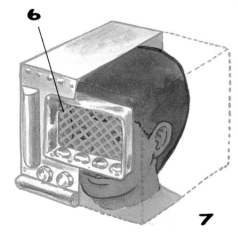

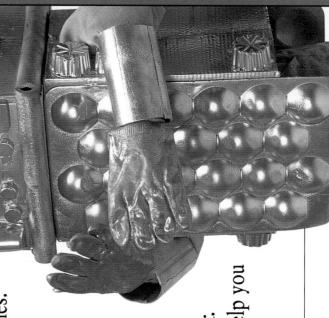

8 Cut the pipe lagging in half and glue around the bottom edge of the box – you could also use empty toilet rolls cut in half through the middle.

9 Tape up the side of the box (**9**). Tape some flat containers onto the sides. If you use rounded shapes, trace and cut around them on the sides and then insert from inside the box. Tape them in place.

10 From one side of the large rectangular box, cut out a hole for your head (same size as **9**). Cut out all of the opposite side. Turn the box to stand on its cut-out side, with the head hole upper-most. Cut out arm holes.

11 Glue the fruit trays onto the front and back, and plastic containers onto the side with the armholes. Paint everything silver.

12 Staple pieces of card into tube shapes for your arms. Paint silver.

13 Paint the gardening gloves and Wellington boots silver.

14 Ask an adult to help you put your costume on.

*Frog*PERSON

Go underwater as a frogperson!

z

★ *2 large plastic bottles; pipe or corrugated tubing; black elastic; old plastic bath mat; swimming goggles; small piece of card; and silver paint.*

Wear track-suit or leggings and a leotard

1 Tape bottles together. Fit plastic tubing onto one bottle neck. Cut a piece off the end and tape this to the other bottle top. Tape this to the large piece of tubing; paint it all silver.

2 For the mouthpiece, cut a hole in the centre of the card. Place the free length of piping through this. Paint it silver and bend the card over slightly.

3 Cut out two flipper shapes from the bath mat. Stick some velcro at the back to attach over bare feet. Ask an adult to tie some elastic between the bottles to fix the outfit to your body.

4 Get your goggles on. Get diving!

z

Other IDEAS

From pirates to mice, try some more costumes.

> ★ *Use baseball caps, felt and fur fabric to make fox, mice and elephant costumes. Use fruit trays for a carnival headdress. Use felt, a plastic bottle and tin foil for the pirate.*

Use the grid patterns for the fox and mouse. Follow stage 2 of the vampire bat for ears *(see page 12)*.

Fox

1 Stitch the fur fabric ears onto the fur fabric headband shape *(see grid)*. Staple these in place on the back of the baseball cap. Stick some cardboard behind the ears to make them stand up.

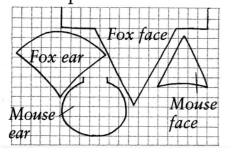

2 Cut straws in half and staple to the nose shape – cut a cotton wool ball in half. Paint this all black and staple onto fur fabric.

Mouse

Follow the steps for the fox, but use grey and pink felt, without a headband shape.

Carnival

Cut a fruit tray into five segments, lengthways (follow the curve of the shapes); staple onto a piece of card. Tape and stitch the card to the headband; decorate with bright colours.

Elephant

Cut out thin foam ears and staple to the side of a grey baseball cap. Stitch some ducting (available from electrical shops) onto the back of the baseball cap – or you can use a "slinky" type toy to make the trunk.

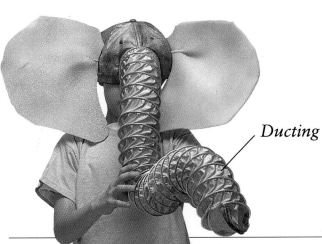

Ducting

Pirate *(see cover)*

Make an eye patch out of black felt; attach it over one eye with elastic. Make a hook out of twisted tinfoil, inserted into the top of a cut off plastic bottle, painted black. Wear jeans and a T-shirt.

Fancy dress WORDS

Gathering stitch This is a large flat stitch used to form gathers.

Grid Squared paper which helps you to copy and enlarge a pattern.

Non-toxic A substance which is not poisonous

Oversewing This is when you sew over two edges.

Scoring This is when you drag scissors across card without cutting it.

Template An outline shape which you draw around to give you an exact copy.

What to do NEXT

If you have enjoyed making costumes, why not have a go at making your own costume designs? There are lots of other books in libraries about design and costume-making to give you ideas.

INDEX

All costumes designed and made by Moe Casey except for cover, both: David West. Photographs by Roger Vlitos except for page 3, top left & bottom right: Eye Ubiquitous; top right: James Davis Travel Photography.